LEGACY EXTRAORDINAIRES

BY

LEGACY SCHOLARS

c/o 2016

YOUNG BREED PUBLICATIONS
INKSTER, MICHIGAN

First Printing: 2017

Cover Design: Bryce Davis

Graphic Designer: Patricia Rasch

Editor(s): LeDeanea Williams, Yvelette Stines & Haneef Sabree

Published by Young Breed Publications, Inkster, MI 48141

Email: 88.hsabree@nhaschools.com
        hjsabree@att.net

Website: jrhandsonsllc.dudaone.com & hjsabree.wix.com/ jrhandsonsllc

Printed in the United States of America

Library Of Congress Control Number: 2017953464

ISBN: 978-0-9846633-2-3

ABOUT THE AUTHOR(S)

- ➤ Represent some of Legacy's brightest young minds

- ➤ Embody the virtues of the Moral Focus

- ➤ Have the potential to make significant positive changes in today's society

- ➤ Ceiling for growth is unparalleled

- ➤ Each scholar has unique and primary talents that when unified results in a rich tapestry]

- ➤ Are proud representatives of Detroit, Michigan, which is home to Legacy Charter Academy (4900 E. Hildale St., 48234, 313.368.2215)

LEGACY CHARTER ACADEMY…..
GO BLUE AND GOLD,
GO TITANS!!!............

WHO ARE WE?.......................

Dedicated to the Class of 2016 from
Legacy Charter Academy and young scholars
around the world.

**One Team
One Goal
One Direction**

TABLE OF CONTENTS

Stories (Opening Scene)

Moral Focus Virtues

Motivational Poems

Scholar's Creed

Middle School Anthem

Finale (Closing scene)

Stories

NO BULLY ZONE!

Writers:

      Asha Martin

      Jayla Reed

      Destiny Walker

      Shakira Thompson

      Kearyana Jenkins

      Dyimond Hall

Chapter 1: What is Bullying?

What is bullying? Bullying is an unwanted aggressive behavior by one or more individuals. Harassing someone is not a good thing to do. This unwanted behavior includes actions, like making threats, spreading rumors, attacking someone physically or verbally, and excluding someone from a group on purpose. Intimidation can happen anywhere. It can happen in your neighborhood, at school, and online.

There are many roles that people can play in bullying. People can bully others, get bullied, or may witness bullying. When people are involved in harassment, they often play more than one role. It is important to understand several roles of bullying, in order to effectively prevent and respond to this behavior.

There are three types of bullying. The types are cyber, physical, and verbal bullying. When people are bullied, they have a hard time standing up for themselves. Bullying can make people feel sad, lonely, or nervous. Also, bullying can make students have trouble in school, like failing classes or skipping classes. Sometimes people follow their friend and bully as a team. That's why it's good to be a leader, not a follower. Bullying isn't good under any circumstances.

Chapter 2: Physical Bullying

Physical bullying is a serious problem. It affects not only the bully and the victim, but also the other students who witness the bullying. Parents, teachers, other concerned adults, and young people should be aware of what physical bullying is. There are many types of negative physical interaction that can occur between young people. This includes fighting, practical jokes, and sexual harassment.

In this context, physical bullying can take many forms: hitting, pushing, tripping, slapping, and spitting. This may include stealing or destroying possessions, such as books, clothing, or lunch money. Physical bullying can cross the line of sexual harassment or sexual assault. Physical bullying occurs often at school. It can also occur on the way to, from, and after school. Victims of physical bullying are usually weaker than the bully, or the victim may be socially marginalized.

Some signs that a student may be a victim of physical bullying include coming home from school with bruises, cuts, or other injuries. On a side note, bullying certainly happens in middle school. Young ladies get bullied too; they are either the perpe-trators or victims of physical bullying. This type of bullying can lead to depression and sometimes suicide. You shouldn't encourage your children to fight back because then they will become the bully. There is a healthy way to stand up to a bully, so there is no further altercation or issues.

Chapter 3: Verbal Bullying

Verbal bullying is something that happens everywhere. For example, it can happen at home, but especially at school. Verbal bullying is something that harms people mentally, not physically. Verbal means harming people with words. For example, name calling, or hurting others feelings with the things that you say. Most people have been a victim of verbal bullying, and have no clue about it. People get their feelings hurt constantly, and fail to address the intimidation correctly.

This happens because they lack the tools necessary to resolve the conflict wisely. Generally, if you're aware it would be obvious if someone was being rude and trying to push you around for no reason. However, in order for it to be bullying it has to be constant, and not provoked. The main part of it has to be one-sided, meaning only the bully is saying rude things, not you.

Verbal bullying has many effects that harm people in many different ways. Most victims feel empty or broken inside. You may feel worthless, but reminding yourself that you are worth everything is important toward persevering through any difficult situation.

Chapter 4: Cyber Bullying

Cyberbullying is bullying that takes place using (electronic) technology. (Electronic) technology includes devices such as cell phones, computers, or tablets; it includes using communication tools, social media sites, text messaging, and chats as well. Examples of cyberbullying include mean text messages or emails, rumors sent by emails, mean things posted on social networking sites, and embarrassing pictures or videos posted.

Neither technology nor social networking sites should be the blame for cyberbullying. Social media sites can or should be used for positive things, like keeping friends and families updated with each other. Completing tasks are now easier and can be done quicker, with the help of technology. The most positive thing about the World Wide Web is it helps us with school related work. But, these same tools can also be used to hurt people. Whether done in person or through technology, the negative effects are similar.

The 2013 – 2014 School Crime Supplement survey indicates that 7% of students in grades 6 – 12 experience cyberbullying. The 2013 Youth Risk Behavior Surveillance Survey finds that 15% of high schoolers were electronically bullied in the past year.

Cyberbullying can happen 24 hours a day, 7 days a week. It can happen at any time of the day or night. Messages and images can be posted anonymously and it spreads quickly to a (very) wide audience. It can be difficult and sometimes impossible to trace the source of harassing messages and texts. It is extremely challenging to stop pictures and videos from being spread, after they have been posted or sent.

Chapter 5: Ways to Prevent Bullying

If you want to prevent bullying, you have to take action and stand up for people who are being bullied. Bullies often want an audience and approval. Maybe you can even take a bullying pledge. Once you take action, that doesn't mean by fighting; that means just take up for the person that's getting bullied. You can take the bullying issues to others, so as a team you can help prevent bullying. Talk to your teachers or principal about what's going on. Maybe your parents or guardians can help by talking to your teachers, principal, or dean.

It might help to write down your feelings and emotions. If you don't want to express your feelings to anyone, writing will help. Speaking up and not being scared towards the bullying, might make your emotions better. If speaking up seems too hard or not safe, just walk away. If the bullying issue leads to fighting, don't fight just walk away; it's not worth it. When you walk away, talk to an adult that you can trust. Keeping your feelings inside will make you feel worse.

Telling someone can help you feel less alone. Keeping your anger inside about the bullying problem, won't help. Be kind to the person that's being bullied. When you see bullying, there are safe things you can do to make it stop. Most bullying happens when adults aren't around.

The kid who is doing the bullying will think it is okay to treat people like that. So when you see somebody bullying someone, take up for them. Don't just stand there, take action. Someone can actually get hurt. Then the person might start to have suicidal thoughts. Let Earth be a bully free zone.

Chapter 6: How to Fix Bullying?

A lot of people in the world have trouble with bullying. Bullying occurs in all grade levels. Entire school districts need to have a language within all the schools in order to fix bullying. To start, all schools need to have a common definition of bullying. Bullying has been a dangerous life-threatening epidemic. Children cannot get away from it, which has led to many suicides. People are struggling to fix bullying, especially in schools.

First, you have to address the behaviors. When addressing the behaviors you have to be nonjudgmental. When teachers and staff call a child a bully or a victim, they are placing a judgment on them. This can cause problems for them in the future. Second, find out what happened before deciding whether or not the incident qualifies as bullying. Keep in mind that each student involved in a situation comes from different circumstances. There might be a reason that the child who engages in behavior characterized as bullying, is acting that way. To fix these problems with bullying, involve the student who's doing the bullying (U.S. Department of Health and Human Services, n.d.).

You can join activities in your school (with other people) to help fix bullying; if your school doesn't have any, you can make up your own. Talk to adults at your school to get permission. You can google groups that you can join too. There are many bullying groups you can join after school. All of the previous steps mentioned can help you fix bullying!

GOING THE DISTANCE...

Chelsey Humphries
Dominique Pitts
Javayla Grant
Dazaira Carter-Harris
Sha'Nya Perdue

"Pancakes! Pancakes! Come and get them before you head out to school!" I hurried down the stairs, almost tripping and falling on my face. Trinity, my three-year-old sister trying to follow after me, is taking each step one by one. I pick her up by her waist and she squeals.

"Quentin! Put me down!" she screams, while laughing. I continue down the stair and put her down in the kitchen, but not before tickling her stomach. I see my mother, and she's putting a huge plate of pancakes down on the counter. My dad walks in with my six-year-old sister, Madison, on his leg and nine-year-old, Chelsea, on his back, laughing. He's dressed in his work clothes.

"Quit playing," my mother says chuckling. "You have a good twenty minutes to eat before you have to go to school," she says. "…. And you, John," addressing my father, as he stuffs another piece of bacon into his mouth.

After he finishes eating, my father approaches the door, saying goodbye to us all. He opens the door; the world outside is unusually black as if filled with smoke. It seeps through the doorway and when it touches my parents, they immediately fall to the ground. I can't breathe clearly; it feels as if my throat is swelling up. I look to the ground to help my parents, but confusingly, they are no longer here.

I shield my sisters, who are coughing and hacking from the smoke. The smoke slowly creeps up the wall, painfully towards us. Somehow I know that if this smoke touches us, we'll end up just like our parents. I turn to run up the stairs with my sisters but the smoke touches my leg. A shooting pain runs up my calf to my spine and then my head. I crumple down to the floor, screaming for my sisters to run, but it seems like all of their feet are glued to the floor.

A hair-raising scream awakens me. I am in my room, covered in a cold sweat. A pair of gentle hands are placed on my biceps. I look to my left and see my little sister Trinity by my bedside with a tear-streaked face. I then realized it was only a dream, much like the others, in which I've been entrapped for the past 2 years, since my mother and father died from that worldwide-ravaging disease.

"Quentin, do you need me to sleep with you again tonight?" It's amazing how a three-year-old doesn't have the slightest nightmare but I have consistent full blown nightmare terrors. I nod, pathetically, and pull the covers so she can get in with me. I hold her as tight as I can, afraid that the plague will catch her. Even though I cannot protect her from it, I tell her I will anyway, and that she will have to protect me, too.

Every time I have this dream it makes me reminisce on the old days when we were able to go to school like normal kids or when there were 7 billion people on the surface of the

Earth.......(or when we weren't orphans like most of my friends now). All I remember is sitting on the couch playing "Call of Duty: Black Ops," when my mother came storming in through the front door, demanding that I turn it off and turn to a news station.

There was an alert to stay indoors because some disease, that I wasn't paying attention to at the time, got brought over from Poland. Apparently people were dropping like flies.

So far, the disease symptoms have not been showing in any of us at all, but even Trinity knows that it's just a matter of time.

The following morning was the same consistent routine as always. I wake my sister from my bed and tell her to get showered and dressed, even though we aren't planning to go anywhere any time soon. We are getting ready for the 'peacekeepers' to come and test us for any early signs of the plague.

We sit in an uncanny silence. We have nothing to say. We're starring at random things in the room when the peacekeepers burst through the door as always without so much as a pause or knock.

There are five of them; I roll my eyes at how they unnecessarily sent five men to test four kids. They all smell like sterile hospitals. They are dressed in all white full body suits, wearing gas masks like the people in "Star Wars."

"Quentin, why do we have to do this every day? My finger is starting to get sore from getting pricked all the time..." Madison whines, while pulling on my pant leg.

The peacekeeper, completely ignoring her, snatches her index finger, pricking it hard with the needle, rigidly processing it through the scanner. She whimpers while wiping the blood away with her thumb. I bend down to face her and see tears threatening to roll down her cheeks.

"Maddie," I begin, seriously, "you know they're just tryin' to keep you safe and healthy, and you know I wouldn't let them do it if that wasn't the case. Anyway, if..." I wasn't able to finish what I was saying because a different peacekeeper came over and abruptly snatched me up, practically stabbing my finger with the needle.

Unconsciously, my instant reflexes forcibly grabbed his arm and pushed, making him stumble back. Once he regained balance, he said, in a raspy voice from behind his mask, "You do realize that could cost you and your family food privileges?"

My hands clench and unclench, trying to control my anger, while I think in my head, "how is eating a privilege?" I was just about to express my thoughts when Trinity grabbed my hand and unclenched it with her small hands. All my anger diminishes and I regain my self-control.

———

"Yes, I do realize that and I'm sorry for my disrespectful actions, sir."

"You are forgiven. You are all free of the virus. God Bless." He replies in a practiced rigid, robotic voice.

They all walk out in a single file line out the door to the next house to repeat the same procedure.

"Thank you Trin. I was just about to lose my temper. If it hadn't been for you, we probably wouldn't have had food for the next 3 days.

She giggles, "Well you can stand to lose a few pounds anyway," she snickers while running away. I know this isn't true because every day before the plague emerged, I went to the gym in our school.

I pressed my hand to my chest and gasped, seemingly offended. I run after her with Madison and Chelsea right behind me, laughing. I follow her into her room, tackle her on the bed, and begin tickling her, making her laugh uncontrollably. As I'm doing this, I suddenly get tackled by Chelsea and Madison, and then Trinity joins in. In this moment, I realize this is the first time that we've ever had real fun since mom and dad died.

It feels good to laugh with them, although this good time we are having will be short lived. Trinity starts to cough violently and runs to the bathroom.

"Trinity, are you okay?" I call after her. I run to the bathroom to see her kneeling over the toilet. I'm thinking that she just threw up, but when I walk over to the toilet I see glistening scarlet red blood on her lips and in the toilet water. All the blood drains from my face as I quickly usher the other two girls out of the bathroom and into the bedroom. They are already starting to cry because they know what I know.

Spewing blood is the first phase of the disease, but, more importantly, it isn't hard to catch because it travels through the air.

I hastily stumble down the stairs, raiding the bottom kitchen cabinet for gas masks. I take the stairs three at a time, trying to prevent anymore sickness. I swiftly put my mask on and then made sure both Madison's and Chelsea's were secure before going to check on Trinity.

"Trinity, are you alright?" I ask cautiously.

"What's happening? Why do you have a mask on, Quentin? And why am I throwing up blood? Quentin what's happening to me?!"

"Trinity I think you might be sick." As soon as I said that she began to wail out and cry immediately.

"It might not be the plague, girlie. It might just be a bug that's going to pass. Think positive…And plus, we haven't gotten it so far, so maybe we are all immune to it." I say sympathetically, hoping she'd believe all the lies that just came out of my mouth. I already know that there is no such luck though.

"Yeah, maybe that's it." She says, eyeing me suspiciously.

"Let's get you to bed." I suggest, as I wipe her mouth with a paper towel. "I'll get your bed ready while you brush your teeth and put on your pajamas. Okay?" She nods somberly and begins to do as she's instructed.

I walk slowly to the guest bedroom, where she's going to sleep from now on. I'm confused as to why the scanner didn't pick up the fact she was sick. She must have had it when they pricked her. Protocol says that I have to immediately notify the peacekeepers so they can take her off on one of the sterile white stretchers to be poked and prodded by doctors and scientists. But…..I have decided……I'm not going to put my little sister through that.

As I finish making the bed, I glance up and see her standing in the doorway, in her purple unicorn pajamas. She's looking confused.

"Why am I sleeping in here instead of in the bed with Maddie and Chels, like I always do? I'm going to be lonely in here by myself!"

"You wouldn't want everyone else to get sick, would you Trin?" She shakes her head no, earnestly. "And in case you get lonely, you can sleep with Harvey." Harvey is her stuffed elephant that she's had ever since she was born; she loves the ratty old thing. She gives me a toothy grin and jumps on the bed.

I tuck her in and reached to turn off the light but she says, "Nooo! Read me a bedtime story so I can go to sleep!"

"Alright, but after that, you have to go to sleep. Which story do you want, Cinderella or Sleeping Beauty?" I ask, even though I already know that she's going to choose the latter.

I start the story off and she's already yawning. I can tell that she's not going to make it through the whole story. Even as she falls asleep in the middle of the story, I keep reading to ensure that she gets a goodnight sleep. After finishing, I turn the lamp out and go to put the

others to bed; but when I get to them, I see they've already gotten their nightclothes on and are in bed asleep.

Whew, (sighing)! This is the first time that I've gotten the chance to relax in a while. Taking full advantage of this, I sat on the couch to watch T.V. The first thing I see when I press the power button is the news, which is not surprising, although what they are showing is quite shocking. The headline says in all caps: 'ANTIDOTE FOUND FOR INFECTIOUS DISEASE!' I'm suddenly very alert; I turn the volume up as high as possible, until its speakers are blaring out words:

"Scientists believe they found an antidote for this virus which has plagued a lot of our loved ones. Scientists at the Edward Lewis Health Center in Lowell, Massachusetts have found an antidote which will be going on the market for sale at $1000.00 per tube."

I stare at the screen not comprehending anymore of what the news lady was saying. We need those antidotes and of course we don't have that type of money just sitting around.

That's when a plan popped into my head! A plan that was probably stupid from the start, but I just had to try it. It could change our lives!

The next morning started out as usual. I woke my sisters up, but this time, I woke them up at five a.m. to set the first stage of the plan into motion.

"Chelsea, come here. " She skipped over to me. It is still surprising to me that she could have this much energy so early. "I called the next-door neighbors. You know Mr. and Mrs. Johnson? Well, they have agreed to take you in for a few days. There's some business that I have to take care of, okay?" She tilted her head in confusion, worry vividly clear in her eyes.

"Where are you going, Quentin? Can I come with you? I promise I won't get in the way."

I chuckled at the thought of how my plan would work out if she actually came with me. "Nope, not this time; but I promise that next time something comes up, you, Trinity and Madison can tag along." She eventually agreed.

I collected all the food that we had and put it in backpacks for each of them. The Johnsons' are aware of Trinity's current health situation, so gas masks will be on 24/7. I was really surprised when they actually agreed to take them all in, especially when the little one probably has contracted the plague. They are probably sympathetic cause' we don't have any parents now. Usually I hate sympathy, but right now, it's coming in handy.

———

I pack their clothes for a maximum of three days. I collect toothpaste, toothbrushes, toilet paper, and other random things. I just don't want them to go over there and use all of the Johnsons' supplies.

I walk them over to the house, nervous that they have changed their minds. I probably would've changed mine. They all go in without saying anything but a simple "hi" and "hello" to the Johnsons. They turn back to me and I get on one knee so I can face them directly. I can tell that they might start to cry any minute.

I look at their gas-masked faces and tell them, "I will be right back in a couple days, you'll barely know I was gone. Trust me... When I get back, you're all going to thank me for what I've done."

Responding to me with silence, I get up and hug them as they all hug me back. I'm amazed at how strong my three little sisters are, even in troubling times like these. "Remember to be respectful to Mr. and Mrs. Johnson and to not cause too much trouble. You know how to fix your own food and to get ready for bed on your own, so you should be fine."

I finally stand up and go for the door and walk out but not before giving the Johnsons an appreciative smile. They nod their heads in return, knowing that what I'm about to do isn't going to be an easy task, but totally necessary.

I take the stairs down to the sidewalk. There is no one outside like always. All I have to watch out for are patrollers because if they catch me, I'll be immediately arrested and sent to a detention facility for a long period of time. At least, that's what I heard.

I start to walk down the street after I put my hood over my head. Surprisingly, the streets were fairly clean except for a few random pieces of paper here and there. I pass houses that I remember as my friends' houses but now they are empty and the few houses that are inhabited have only a few residents. The journey after that starts to become plain. I'm not thinking I just take a left turn here, and a right turn there. Once I actually got lost and had to retrace my steps.

I stop in front of a building and it takes me a while to regain attention to my surroundings. I have arrived at Edward Lewis Health Center, which is only 2 miles from my house. I take out a ski mask and slip it over my head, over the gas mask. Here goes nothing.

Everything that I remember about this place is helping me out tremendously right now. I remember when my mom was having all three of the girls. We came here and I got to explore the spacious hospital/research center. I remember vaguely traveling all the way to the top floor and seeing a whole bunch of scientist mixing and swirling different types of what looked like antidotes. One scientist finally saw me looking through the doorway and started shouting, appearing to panic. Others then began to notice my presence and do the same thing. They finally escorted me out and assured me that everything is fine and nothing was going on.

I'm sure that secretive floor is where they keep the antidotes, so that's where I'm headed.

I start by walking directly through the double doors of the hospital. Nobody's in the lobby but a security guard at the front, who's asleep, and a woman at the desk, who is talking on the phone about something that seems to be very important. I look to my right, and there are two white doors where I remember them being. I go into the second door, remembering it leads to a staircase, which will take me all the way up to the top floor.

I start to climb the stairs but, at every floor level, there's an elevator door. When I reached the third floor, the top of the elevator door started to ping, letting me know that someone would get off at this level soon. I look for a way out, knowing that trying to go back down the stairs would get me caught. I look to my left and see a vent with no grate to it. This particular vent looks like it will be able to fit me perfectly, so I decide 'what the heck?' I bend down and shuffle my way into the vent, sure it's a tight squeeze but I have no other choice. Once I'm in, I hear the elevator open. I stop breathing, literally. I hear men talking in a very formal manner about different components of something. Then suddenly, I hear one say something about the grate being off.

He then puts the grate back on and screws it back in, very tight. I know because I am, as you read, now making several attempts to kick it back off again, but it just won't budge.

Finally deciding to venture forward into the vents, I find another open grate and crawl through it.

I look around and realize that I'm in someone's office and it's currently in use.

"Yes, Mr. Brandon, the antidote has been tested on numerous test subjects that have contracted the virus."

"And, tell me," Mr. Brandon asks in response, "what happened to those patients that you have tested?" Meanwhile I'm sitting in the corner unnoticed, panicking, trying to formulate a plan of getting out of here. If I try to go back through the vent, surely they will hear me. I continue listening.

"Every person that took the antidote became well within the 24 hours of it being taken. Even those who were in the last and final stage of the virus recovered from it. I must say your idea came in handy while making this product."

"Well, I'm glad it did. Now why don't you take me to go see these miracle patients that you've cured?" Mr. Brandon asked in a superior way, oozing confidence in the way he spoke.

"Certainly sir, right this way." I hear footsteps and the door opens then closes. I am finally able to breathe now, shoulders relaxing, as all the tension is going out from them.

I stood up off the ground, looking around. I see stubbed out cigars in the cigarette tray and Scotch in small glasses in between two big leather chairs. Something else caught my interest though. It was a big leather bound journal sitting on a huge oak desk towards the back of the office. I walked towards it, picked it up and opened it. The first words I read were: 'we shouldn't have let out the disease.'

I immediately slam the book shut, my breaths suddenly turning ragged. I can't believe what I just read. I look to the cover and it says Carlton Brandon: Daily Journal Entries. Why would he dare leave this out in the open? I stand there thinking for about a minute. The hospital that found the cure is the one that let the disease out in the first place. I would bet on my life that all of this was for money, especially when they are charging $1,000 bucks for one dose.

Snapping out of my thoughts and into focus, I slip the journal into my backpack and return to my mission. I peak my head out of the door that the men just went through and see that no one is there. I take the opportunity and run out, heading back to the stairs. Finally, I make it to the top floor, uninterrupted! I hesitate at the final double doors, thinking to myself, 'do I really want to do this?' My immediate answer is "yes", and I bust through the doors.

I rush in and everyone jumps back. Surprisingly, there is no security in the room, just skinny, scientists. I grab the nearest scientist and take the cutting knife from my pocket that I brought earlier, pressing his back to my chest with the knife to his throat. I can easily overpower him. I have about 5 inches on him, being 6' 3, along with a 60-pound advantage.

"Show me where the antidotes are and I don't hurt anyone in this room!" I shout very loudly. Nobody moves when I say this, so to get them moving, I growl out, "NOW!!!!!"

One very pale looking woman in a long lab coat turns to grab something with her bony hands. I immediately go to hide. There's a big freezer next to me, so I open it and get in, dragging the scientist I'm holding with me. Sure enough it was a gun. Shots were being fired directly at the freezer, leaving nothing but a dent, as the freezer was made of metal. I quickly look behind me and there are vials of different color liquids.

"Are there any cures in here?" I ask the man. He nods 'yes'.

"Which color is the right one, green, purple or blue?" I feel his Adam's apple bobbing up and down against the knife, struggling to answer. I pull the knife away a bit.

"The antidotes are the green ones. The other colors are failed inventions that we like to keep." He says this in a shaky voice. Meanwhile, I hear shouts and orders coming from outside, no one daring to try and open the freezer (doors).

———

I fill my backpack with all the green vials that could fit. "These better be the right color or I promise I will come back and you won't get to enjoy any of the money you were promised," I whisper the threat in his ear, emphasizing it by pressing the knife harder to his throat. He nods and gulps.

"I swear it's the right color, please just don't kill me," he pleads that it's time to go out.

Not wasting any time, I bust through the freezer doors with the scientists still in my clutches. Six guns greet me when I come out. Feeling that I have no choice, I let go of the man and drop my knife. I still have the big backpack on my shoulder. As they slowly start to move in, I see a thin window to the left and make a sudden decision to jump. No one was expecting that. Thinking that I fell, I hear them all running down to the stairs, not knowing that I had grabbed the ledge and swung into the window below the one I jumped out of. I secretly thank my mom for forcing me to go to gymnastics when I was in 5th grade.

I waste no time in taking the back stairs, jumping three at a time, it takes no time at all to reach the first floor.

The lobby woman is yelling after me like I was really going to stop. The security guard is very much awake now but I'm much bigger than him so I just shoved him to the floor.

I take off down the street faster than Usain Bolt, running the whole two miles it takes to get home, hearing sirens getting farther away, but I know they'll catch up to me.

I jump up the five stairs to the Johnsons' house and pound on the door hard. Mrs. Johnson opens the door and gasps at my appearance. I take off the ski mask and she breathes a breath of relief.

"Each one of you, take one of the vials in here, only one!" I instruct her while handing over the backpack. "It will keep you healthy so you cannot contract the disease. Give one to anyone you know or see." Then my sisters come up behind her. "Remember that I love you very much! Be strong!" I say, looking each of them straight in the eyes.

"Get back into the house! You never saw me! Hide those vials in the safest place you can find!"

With that, I grab the doorknob and slam the door shut. I run down the stairs hastily, now that the sirens are just 1 block away. I run into a huge abandoned building, further down the way and across street, trying to stay hidden. The sirens get louder and I feel like I'm about to pass out, when they finally pass the building that I'm in.

I will never be able to go back to my family, not if I don't want them to end up with the same fate as me.

According to the wanted posters put up the next day, I'm officially classified as a fugitive. The patrollers have doubled since I escaped, and the peacekeepers went to each neighborhood door, explaining what happened, telling everyone to be on the lookout.

As long as Trinity, Madison, and Chelsea are well and safe, with my destiny, I am at peace...............

Moral Focus

Virtues

Motivational
Poems

The Disaster of Negative Thinking

If you think you are beaten, you are
If you think you dare not, you don't,
If you like to win, but think you can't
It is almost certain that you won't.

If you think you'll lose, you've lost
For out in the world we find,
Success begins with a fellow's will
It's all in the state of mind.

If you think you are outclassed, you are
You've got to think high to rise,
You've got to be sure of yourself before
You can ever capture the prize.

Life's battles don't always go
To the stronger or faster man*,
But sooner or later the man who wins
Is the man WHO THINKS THAT HE CAN!

-Author unknown

---

* man/woman, he/she

Equipment

Figure it out for yourself, my lad,
You've all that the greatest of men* have had,
Two arms, two hands, two legs, two eyes,
And a brain to use if you would be wise.
With this equipment they all began,
So start for the top and say 'I can.'

Look them over, the wise and great,
They take their food from a common plate
And similar knives and forks they use,
With similar laces they tie their shoes,
The world considers them brave and smart.
But you've all they had when they made their start.

You can triumph and come to skill,
You can be great if only you will,
You're well equipped for what fight you choose,
You have legs and arms and a brain to use,
And the man who has risen, great deeds to do
Began his life with no more than you.

You are the handicap you must face,
You are the one who must choose your place,
You must say where you want to go.
How much you will study the truth to know,
God has equipped you for life, But He
Lets you decide what you want to be.

_____

* men/women, man/woman, his/her

Courage must come from the soul within,
The man must furnish the will to win,
So figure it out for yourself, my lad,
You were born with all that the great have had,
With your equipment they all began.
Get hold of yourself, and say: 'I can.'

— Edgar Albert Guest

It Couldn't Be Done
By Edgar Albert Guest

Somebody said that it couldn't be done
    But he with a chuckle replied
That "maybe it couldn't," but he* would be one
    Who wouldn't say so till he'd tried.
So he buckled right in with the trace of a grin
    On his face. If he worried he hid it.
He started to sing as he tackled the thing
    That couldn't be done, and he did it!

Somebody scoffed: "Oh, you'll never do that;
    At least no one ever has done it;"
But he took off his coat and he took off his hat
    And the first thing we knew he'd begun it.
With a lift of his chin and a bit of a grin,
    Without any doubting or quiddit,
He started to sing as he tackled the thing
    That couldn't be done, and he did it.

There are thousands to tell you it cannot be done,
    There are thousands to prophesy failure,
There are thousands to point out to you one by one,
    The dangers that wait to assail you.
But just buckle right in with a bit of a grin,
    Just take off your coat and go to it;
Just start to sing as you tackle the thing
    That "cannot be done," and you'll do it.

————————

* he/she, he'd/she'd, his/her

What Do You Make?

Dinner guests were sitting around the table discussing life. One man, a CEO and hotshot rocket scientist type, decided to explain the problem with education. He argued: "What's a kid going to learn from someone who decided his best option in life was to become a teacher?"

He reminded the other dinner guests that it's true what they say about teachers: "Those who can, do. Those who can't, teach."

To corroborate, he said to another guest: "You're a teacher, Shirley, " he said. "Be honest. What do you make?"

Shirley, who had a reputation of honesty and frankness, replied, "You want to know what I make?"

"I make kids work harder than they ever thought they could. I can make a C+ feel like the Congressional Medal of Honor, and an A- feel like a slap in the face if the student did not do his or her very best.

"I can make kids sit through 40 minutes of study hall in absolute silence.

"I can make parents tremble in fear when I call home.

"You want to know what I make?" "I make kids wonder. I make them question: I make them criticize. I make them apologize and mean it.

"I make them write. I make them read, read, read. I make them spell 'definitely and beautiful' over and over again, until they will never misspell either one of those words again.. I make them show all their work in math and hide it all on their final drafts in English.

"I elevate them to experience music and art and the joy in performance, so their lives are rich, full of kindness and culture, and they take pride in themselves and their accomplishments. I make them understand that if you have the brains, then follow your heart…and if someone ever tries to judge you by what you make, you pay them no attention.

"You want to know what I make? I make a difference.

"What do you make?"

—Author unknown

Worst Day Ever?
By *Chanie Gorkin*

Today was the absolute worst day ever
And don't try to convince me that
There's something good in every day
Because, when you take a closer look,
The world is a pretty evil place.
Even if
Some goodness does shine through once in a while
Satisfaction and happiness don't last.
And it's not true that
It's all in the mind and heart
Because
True happiness can be attained
Only if one's surroundings are good
It's not true that good exists
I'm sure you can agree that
The reality
Creates
My attitude
It's all beyond my control
And you'll never in a million years hear me say
Today was a very good day

NOW READ IT FROM BOTTOM TO TOP, THE OTHER WAY,
AND SEE WHAT I REALLY FEEL ABOUT MY DAY.

Scholar Creed

I am a Legacy Scholar.

I commit to giving effort because it creates

ability and success.

I strive to reach my full potential EVERY DAY.

I exemplify moral character in my words

and my actions.

I work diligently to prepare for my future,

because I am….

"Building A Legacy."

—Leadership Team

Middle School Anthem

IT'S 8 IN THE MORNING,
SCHOLARS ARE YOU ALERT,
TUCK IN YOUR SHIRT,
TUCK IN YOUR SHIRT,

RENDITION DONE WITH EASE,
LEARNING POSITION 1-2-3......
HERE COMES MR. T,
TUCK IN YOUR SHIRT,
TUCK IN YOUR SHIRT.

IT'S 8 IN THE MORNING,
SCHOLARS ARE YOU ALERT,
TUCK IN YOUR SHIRT,
TUCK IN YOUR SHIRT,

RENDITION DONE WITH EASE,
LEARNING POSITION 1-2-3.......
HERE COMES MR. T,
EDUCATION IS THE KEY,
TUCK IN YOUR SHIRT,
TUCK IN YOUR SHIRT.

By: Ms. R. Robinson, Ms. Norfleet –Alderson, Ms. Staley, Ms. Riles, Mr. Tomlinson and Mr. Sabree

Finale
(Epilogue)

ACKNOWLEDGMENTS

Chelsey Humphries, Dominique Pitts, Javayla Grant, Dazaira Carter-Harris, Sha'Nya Perdue, Asha Martin, Jayla Reed, Destiny Walker, Shakira Thompson, Kearyana Jenkins, Dyimond Hall, Mr. Carey, Mr. Tomlinson, Mr. Murphy, Ms. Huckleby, Mr. Little, Mrs. Lupo, Mrs. Weigle, Ms. Upshaw, Ms. M. Robinson, Mrs. Norflleet-Alderson, Ms. R. Robinson, Ms. Latta, Mrs. Dorsey, Ms. McCord, Ms. Brown, Ms. Sweetnich, Mrs. Rezanka, Ms. Barrett, Ms. Thomas, Ms. Bascom, Ms. Riles, Ms. Williams, Ms. Stines and Mr. Sabree

(MIDDLE SCHOOL ROCKS!!!)

LEGACY SCHOLARS!!

*continuation from the beginning of literature

As you maneuver through life remember that when you fail that doesn't make you a failure; it's only through failure that the authenticity of success can be attained. Secondly, often it is not a matter of if you can or you can't, but if you will or you won't. Furthermore, the limitations that you have in this world, will originate from the perceptions of your own mind. Whatever you do make sure to THINK, before you move.

THE KEYS TO SUCCESS:
In school and in life

— Always remember there is but one God….

— Treat others as you'd have others do unto you…principles, character and integrity….

— Take care of business…shoot for the stars….

— Have fun…never allow yourself to be transported by someone who has been drinking or has been using drugs, get "high" on life….

— Date… it's normal….

— Chill with friends….

— Stay active… work out, participate in extra curriculum activities….

— Just plain relax…draw, read for enjoyment….

— Stay healthy…proper nutrition (three good meals a day, adequate hydration, etc.) and proper sleep (eight hours each night is best)…

NOTES

NOTES

NOTES

NOTES

NOTES